DEPARTMENT OF THE NAVY
HEADQUARTERS UNITED STATES MARINE CORPS
3000 MARINE CORPS PENTAGON
WASHINGTON, DC 20350-3000

I0500626

MARINE CORPS FIRE PROTECTION AND EMERGENCY SERVICES PROGRAM

DEPARTMENT OF THE NAVY
HEADQUARTERS UNITED STATES MARINE CORPS
3000 MARINE CORPS PENTAGON
WASHINGTON, DC 20350-3000

MCO 11000.11
LFF-1
23 Jun 2010

MARINE CORPS ORDER 11000.11

From: Commandant of the Marine Corps
To: Distribution List

Subj: MARINE CORPS FIRE PROTECTION AND EMERGENCY SERVICES PROGRAM

Ref: (a) National Fire Protection Association (NFPA), "National Fire Codes" (NOTAL)
      (b) Unified Facilities Criteria (UFC) 3-600-01, "Fire Protection Engineering for Facilities," September 26, 2006
      (c) DODI 6055.06, "DOD Fire and Emergency Services (F&ES) Program," December 21, 2006
      (d) DODI 6055.05, "Occupational and Environmental Health," November 11, 2008
      (e) DOD 6055.05-M, "Occupational Medical Examinations and Surveillance Manual," May 2, 2007 with Change 1, September 16, 2008
      (f) NEHC-Technical Manual (NEHC-TM) OM 6260, "Medical Surveillance Procedures Manual and Medical Matrix (Edition 9)," August 2007
      (g) DOD 6055.06-M, "DOD Fire and Emergency Services Certification Program," February 23, 2006
      (h) Unified Facilities Criteria (UFC) 4-730-10, "Fire Stations," June 15, 2006
      (i) SECNAV M-5214.1
      (j) SECNAV M-5210.1
      (k) SECNAV Instruction 5211.5E
      (l) DOD Directive 3025.1, "Military Support to Civil Authorities (MSCA)," January 15, 1993
      (m) DOD Instruction 2000.18, "Department of Defense Installation Chemical, Biological, Radiological, Nuclear and High-Yield Explosive Emergency Response Guidelines," December 4, 2002
      (n) 29 CFR 1910.146
      (o) Commission on Fire Accreditation International (CFAI), "Fire and Emergency Services Self Assessment Manual," 7th Ed.
      (p) Homeland Security Presidential Directive (HSPD) 5, "Management of Domestic Incidents," February 28, 2003
      (q) 29 CFR 1910.120
      (r) MCO P11000.5G
      (s) Unified Facilities Criteria (UFC) 3-600-02, "O&M: Inspection, Testing and Maintenance of Fire Protection Systems," January 1, 2001
      (t) Fire Administration Authorization Act of 1992
      (u) Naval Air Systems Command, "Naval Air Training and Operating Procedures Standardization (NATOPS) 00-80R-14, U.S. Navy Aircraft Firefighting and Rescue Manual," January 15, 2008
      (v) MCO P3500.67
      (w) DOD Instruction 6055.1, "DOD Safety and Occupational Health (SOH) Program," August 19, 1998
      (x) 40 CFR 300

Encl: (1) Marine Corps Fire Protection and Emergency Services Procedural Manual

Reports Required: I.   Fire and Emergency Services Department Program Assessments (Report Control Symbol Exempt) encl (1), chap. 1, par. 20
                II. Fire Protection Engineering Surveys (Report Control Symbol Exempt) encl (1), chap. 5, par. 2
             III. National Fire Incident Reporting System (NFIRS) (Report Control Symbol DD-1320-01, chap. 7, par. 1
             IV. Large Loss Initial Incident Report ((Report Control Symbol DD-11320-04) (External RCS DD-AT&L(AR)1765)), encl (1), chap. 7, par. 2, App D

1. <u>Situation</u>. To provide policy and procedures, and assign responsibilities governing the Marine Corps Installation Fire Protection and Emergency Services Program per references (a) through (x).

2. <u>Cancellation</u>. MCO P11000.11B.

3. <u>Mission</u>. This Order provides policy to protect Marine Corps personnel and the public from loss of life, injury and illness due to fires and other emergencies as a result of installation activities, aircraft operations, disasters or terrorist incidents. This Order also encourages measures to prevent or minimize damage to Marine Corps property and the environment.

4. <u>Execution</u>

   a. <u>Commander's Intent and Concept of Operations</u>

      (1) <u>Commander's Intent</u>

         (a) Each Marine Corps installation will establish and maintain an effective and efficient fire protection and emergency services program that incorporates fire prevention and public fire education; fire protection engineering; all-hazards emergency response; and fire protection systems inspection, testing and maintenance. Detailed definitions, policy and procedures are contained in the enclosure.

         (b) Each Marine Corps Air Station/Air Facility and Marine Wing Support Squadron (MWSS) will establish and maintain an effective and efficient Aircraft Rescue and Fire Fighting (ARFF) program that incorporates immediate response to aircraft emergencies, hazardous materials emergency response and aircraft fire suppression. Marine Corps ARFF Fire and Emergency Services Departments may also provide support to the installation or local fire and emergency service departments. Detailed procedures for the ARFF program are contained in the enclosure.

         (c) Commanders will ensure the fire protection and emergency services program enhances Marine Corps mission capability by protecting installations and aircraft through preventative risk management, education, emergency response and risk communication.

      (2) <u>Concept of Operations</u>

         (a) All fire and emergency services personnel are properly trained and certified for their assigned missions.

(b) All installation facilities are surveyed to identify and correct or control fire and life safety hazards.

(c) All fire protection systems are inspected, tested and maintained to ensure operational readiness.

(d) All facility design, repair and construction projects incorporate required life safety and fire protection engineering standards.

(e) All installation fire and emergency services departments define and document their scope of services and are staffed, equipped and trained to meet the assigned services.

(f) All installation fire and emergency services departments utilize mutual aid agreements with local jurisdictions where the agreements will enhance emergency response capabilities.

(g) All installation fire and emergency services departments develop and provide public fire and injury prevention education programs to motivate installation personnel and families on their fire and injury prevention responsibilities.

(h) All air stations/air facilities and MWSSs maintain an ARFF capability that is staffed, equipped and trained to meet assigned mission.

b. Subordinate Element Tasks

(1) Deputy Commandant for Installations and Logistics. The Deputy Commandant for Installations and Logistics has overall responsibility for installation management including the fire protection and emergency services program and replacement of installation fire and emergency services and ARFF apparatus.

(2) Deputy Commandant for Aviation. The Deputy Commandant for Aviation has overall responsibility for the ARFF program on Marine Corps Air Stations/Air Facilities and in the MWSSs.

(3) Installation/Air Station/MWSS Commanders

(a) Commanders are responsible for establishing and maintaining a comprehensive and effective fire protection and emergency services and/or ARFF program at the installations, activities and facilities under their control.

(b) Installation commanders shall ensure Fire Chiefs, ARFF officers in charge (OICs) and senior Fire and Emergency Services Department officers have direct access to the commander.

(4) Installation Fire Chief. The Fire Chief serves as the senior fire protection manager and technical representative to the installation commander. The Fire Chief is responsible for the direct management and organization of the installation fire and emergency services department.

(5) ARFF Officer in Charge (OIC). The ARFF OIC serves as the senior ARFF manager and ARFF technical representative to the Air Station or MWSS commander. The ARFF OIC is responsible for the direct management and organization of the Air Station or MWSS ARFF Section.

(6) Reserve Activities

(a) Reserve activity commanders are responsible for establishing and maintaining an effective fire protection and emergency services program at the activities and facilities under their control.

(b) Since emergency response services are generally provided by outside forces, the reserve program shall focus on fire prevention practices, first aid fire fighting and public fire education efforts. Reserve activity commanders shall ensure emergency response agreements are in place with outside municipal, district or governmental agencies to provide emergency response services.

c. Coordinating Instructions. Submit recommendations concerning the fire protection and emergency services program to the Commandant of the Marine Corps (CMC) (LFF-1); recommendations on the ARFF program shall be submitted to CMC (APX-34).

5. Administration and Logistics

a. This Order is applicable to all Marine Corps Installations, Air Stations/Air Facilities, MWSSs and includes non-appropriated fund activities and operations under the sponsorship of the Marine Corps Community Services (MCCS) program.

b. Commanders shall ensure adequate staff and budget are provided to implement the fire protection and emergency services and ARFF programs of this Order.

c. Commanders shall prepare local fire protection regulations and instructions which implement this Order at their installation. Such guidance shall be consistent with this Order, but may be more detailed to meet local conditions.

d. Tenant commands and activities located on Marine Corps installations shall adhere to this Order. Marine Corps commands or units located on other DoD or Service installations shall adhere to the host command's fire protection and emergency service standards.

6. Command and Signal

a. Command. This Order is applicable to the Marine Corps Total Force.

b. Signal. This Order is effective the date signed.

J. WILLIAMS
Director, Marine Corps Staff

DISTRIBUTION: PCN 10211300800

Marine Corps
Fire Protection
and
Emergency Services
Procedural Manual

RECORD OF CHANGES

Log completed change action as indicated

Change Number	Date of Change	Date Entered	Signature of Person Incorporating Change

TABLE OF CONTENTS

Chapter 1

Fire Protection and Emergency Services Management

1. <u>Standards</u>. The Marine Corps has adopted the relevant codes and standards of reference (a) and reference (b) as minimum fire protection and emergency services requirements.

2. <u>Requirements</u>. The requirements presented herein are minimum requirements and shall not be reduced until all available alternatives to eliminate deficiencies have been exhausted. In determining the fire protection and emergency services requirements, the following factors shall be considered.

   a. Strategic importance and mission criticality of the installation.

   b. Degree of fire and life safety hazards.

   c. Value at risk (facilities, equipment, contents).

   d. Extent of automatic protection provided.

   e. Availability of outside support.

   f. Emergency response requirements (emergency medical services, hazardous materials response, specialized rescue, disaster response).

3. <u>Deviations</u>. Short-term deviations to the requirements contained in this Order, consistent with reference (c) and lasting less than 90 days, are permitted. The Installation Commander has the authority to approve short-term deviations. Temporary deviations, consistent with reference (c) and lasting longer than 90 days but less than 365 days, are permitted. The authority to approve temporary deviations is held by the echelon commander in the direct chain of command of, and one level higher than, the installation commander (i.e. Commanding General, Marine Corps Installations East; Commanding General Marine Corps Installations West, etc.). A copy of all approved short-term and temporary deviations shall be forwarded to CMC (LFF). Requests for long-term deviations, consistent with reference (c) and that are not expected to be remedied, shall be forwarded to CMC (LFF) for consideration. CMC (LFF) is the first line of authority for approval of long-term deviations to this Order, in accordance with reference (c). Requests for long-term deviations shall be fully justified and include an appropriate risk analysis and risk communication strategy, and include all documentation required by reference (c). Request for long-term deviations forwarded to CMC (LFF) must include endorsement by all management levels (echelon commanders) in the direct chain of command of the requesting installation.

4. <u>Classification</u>. A Fire Protection and Emergency Services Program classification system shall be utilized to determine the level of protection required at an individual Marine Corps installation. The classification rating is based on the factors discussed in paragraph 2.

   a. <u>Class A</u>: The installation has high strategic importance and is critical to the military readiness of the Marine Corps. The value of property and equipment is high and significant life safety hazards are present. Class A installations require a fire and emergency services force which meets the Minimum Level of Service Objectives - Operations for a Full Alarm Assignment per reference (c), Table E3.T1.

b. <u>Class B</u>: The installation is less critical in strategic importance and military readiness. The value of property and equipment is not as significant as Class A installations and the life safety hazards are reduced. Class B installations require a fire fighting and emergency services force which meets the Minimum Level of Service Objectives – Operations for a First Arriving Company per reference (c), Table E3.T1.

c. <u>Class C</u>: Due its reduced strategic importance and impact to military readiness, as well as its size, location and the availability of outside forces, the installation does not require an organized fire fighting and emergency services force. Class C installations do not require a fire fighting and emergency services force that meets the Minimum Level of Service Objectives – Operations for any program element established in reference (c), Table E3.T1. Class C installations may establish an on-site fire brigade in accordance with reference (c), where outside forces are not available.

5. <u>Fire Flow</u>. The fire flow is used to determine hose stream demands and durations in target hazards which represents large fire loss potential. The fire flow shall be calculated in accordance with reference (b) for all target hazards. For facilities protected with automatic sprinklers, the fire flow demand is based solely on the hose stream requirement for the occupancy classification. Fire and emergency services departments shall ensure the fire flow demand can be met for target hazards utilizing both in-house and outside resources.

6. <u>Response Times</u>. Fire and emergency services departments shall be strategically located to provide rapid responses to fires and other emergencies. Fire and Emergency Services Department response times to a given fire area shall be in accordance with Minimum Level of Service Objectives – Operations established in reference (c), Table E3.T1. Response times shall be via the shortest practical route and shall take into account traffic conditions or physical obstructions which may increase response times.

7. <u>Outside Fire and Emergency Services Forces</u>. The number of emergency response personnel and equipment needed at any installation depends on the availability of outside forces. Credit for outside forces shall be permitted on a company by company basis when the outside forces conform favorably to the standards prescribed in this Order and existing mutual or automatic aid agreements are in place. For Class A installations, outside forces shall not exceed one-half of the total Fire and Emergency Services Department company requirements. For Class B and Class C installations, no limit shall be placed on the ratio of outside forces versus organic forces used to meet the requirements of reference (c).

8. <u>Fire and Emergency Services Department Staffing</u>. Figures 1-1, 1-2 and 1-3 provide the staffing standards for administration and management, fire prevention, and emergency response personnel. Emergency response staffing standards are based on full-time career personnel working 72 hours per week on 24 hour shifts. The number of emergency response personnel authorized in each Fire and Emergency Services Department is based on the Minimum Level of Service Objectives - Operations for the installation, per reference (c). The number of fire prevention personnel authorized is based on the size of the installation and the Minimum Level of Service Objectives – Prevention, per reference (c). The administrative and management authorizations are based on the overall size of the Fire and Emergency Services Department and the Minimum Level of Service Objectives – Management, per reference (c).

a. Administrative and Management Personnel. The installation Fire Chief provides senior management of the fire and emergency services department and is responsible for enforcing the fire protection program regulations and developing the fire and emergency services department standard operating procedures. The installation Fire Chief shall have direct access to the installation commander. Where authorized, the Assistant Fire Chief of Operations (Shift Supervisor) supervises and trains the assigned emergency response shift and is assigned as the Incident Commander until relieved by the Fire Chief or Deputy Fire Chief. The Deputy Fire Chief or the Assistant Fire Chief of Operations performs the duties of the Fire Chief in his or her absence. Where authorized, the Assistant Fire Chief of Fire Prevention, the Assistant Fire Chief of Training and the Assistant Fire Chief of Emergency Medical Service (EMS) manage the prevention, training and EMS programs respectively.

b. Fire Prevention Personnel. Technically qualified fire prevention personnel conduct fire protection inspections, manage the public education program, review installation construction plans and specifications, investigate fires, provide hazardous operations permits, provide fire protection training and conduct fire protection system acceptance tests. Fire prevention personnel may be utilized to support emergency response operations and supplement emergency response personnel provided appropriate emergency response qualifications are maintained.

c. Emergency Response Personnel. Emergency response personnel positions are covered under OPM Classification GS-0081 or NSPS Investigative and Protective Services Career Group. Emergency response personnel are primarily responsible for performing hazardous fire fighting and emergency services missions. Emergency response personnel shall undergo pre-placement, annual and periodic occupational medical examinations and participate in a medical surveillance program in accordance with references (c), (d), (e) and (f), and shall fully participate in a fire and emergency services fitness and wellness program in accordance with reference (c).

POSITIONS	NUMBER OF FIRE AND EMERGENCY SERVICES DEPARTMENT PERSONNEL 1/
Fire Chief	10 or more = 1
Deputy Fire Chief	40 or more = 1
Assistant Fire Chief (Operations - Shift Supervisor)	20 or more = 2 2/
Assistant Fire Chief (Fire Prevention)	4 or more prevention personnel = 1
Assistant Fire Chief (Training)	30 or more personnel = 1
Assistant Fire Chief (Emergency Medical Service)	8 or more paramedic personnel = 1 3/
Administrative Assistant	40 or more = 1

Notes:

1/ Figures do not consider personnel assigned for fire and emergency service telecommunications, maintenance of fire protection systems or other auxiliary personnel assigned to the Fire and Emergency Services Department.

2/ Additional shift supervisors (District/Battalion Chiefs) are authorized at large or consolidated installations where the physical dispersion of Fire and Emergency Services Department stations makes it unmanageable for one shift supervisor to provide immediate direction of day-to-day operations.

3/ Ability to hire A/C (EMS) requires approval by CMC (LFF).

Figure 1-1.--Minimum Staffing Requirements for Management and Administrative Fire and Emergency Services Department Positions

AREA REQUIRING FIRE PREVENTION SERVICES (IN THOUSANDS OF SQ. FT.) 1/	STAFFING REQUIREMENTS 2/
0-500	0
501-1,000	1
1,001-3,000	2
3,001-5,000	3
5,001-8,000	4
8,001-11,000	5
11,001-14,000	6
14,001-17,000	7
17,001-20,000	8
20,001 and above	3/

1/   Total square footage of buildings (excluding family housing), continuously used outside storage areas (continuous movement of equipment and/or supplies to and from the storage site), ships, and waterfront facilities.

2/   These baseline staffing figures may be increased or decreased depending on the assessment of the hazardous nature of the material stored or operations conducted, amount of emergency response personnel inspections conducted on low hazard occupancies, the mission criticality of the equipment and operations, predominant construction features, utilization of fire prevention personnel for public fire education and review of construction plans, and other local factors bearing on the demand for full-time fire prevention personnel.

3/   Where fire prevention services are required for areas exceeding 20,000,000 square feet, a fire protection specialist is authorized. An additional fire prevention position is authorized for each additional 3,000,000 square feet.

Figure 1-2.--Minimum Staffing Requirements for Fire Prevention Positions

EMERGENCY VEHICLE IDENTIFIERS	STAFFING PER VEHICLE 1/
Pumpers	4
Aerial Ladders/Quints	4
Rescue Apparatus	2 2/
Wildland Fire Apparatus	2 3/
Ambulances	2

1/ Total emergency response staffing is determined by multiplying the required daily staffing of all staffed apparatus by the position staffing factor, 2.72 percent.

2/ Rescue apparatus shall be cross staffed from the pumper positions. Where the hazard and risk warrants, two positions per rescue apparatus may be authorized when approved by HQMC (LFF).

3/ Wildland apparatus is cross staffed from the pumper positions. At installations with severe wildland fire risks, two positions per wildland fire apparatus may be authorized when approved by HQMC (LFF).

Figure 1-3.--Minimum Daily Staffing Requirements for Emergency Response

9. <u>Fire and Emergency Services Telecommunications</u>. Installations shall provide and maintain around-the-clock capability to handle fire and emergency service communications. Telecommunications operators shall be trained in the proper use of communications equipment including telephone, radio, computer aided dispatch, and alarm receiving systems. Operators must be trained for dispatching emergency apparatus and requesting outside assistance as required. Dedicated public safety or equivalent communications specialists are required and telecommunications operators shall be trained and certified at Telecommunicator I or II per reference (g). Bilingual language capability is required at overseas locations. Consolidation of all emergency communications systems at installations is recommended. The number of on-duty communications operators required is based on the performance requirements of Standard 1221 of reference (a) as follows.

a. Ninety-five percent of alarms received on emergency lines shall be answered within 15 seconds, and 99 percent of alarms shall be answered within 40 seconds.

b. Ninety-five percent of emergency call processing and dispatching shall be completed within 60 seconds, and 99 percent of call processing and dispatching shall be completed within 90 seconds.

c. Communications centers that provide emergency medical dispatching protocols shall have at least two telecommunicators on duty at all times.

Enclosure (1)

10. <u>Fire and Emergency Services Department Facilities</u>. Fire stations shall provide a safe and healthy living environment for personnel who occupy the facility on a 24-hour basis. Facilities shall be designed and planned in accordance with reference (h).

11. <u>Fire and Emergency Services Department Vehicles and Support</u>. Fire and emergency services department emergency vehicles shall be programmed and purchased via HQMC (LFS). Support vehicles shall be provided for command and fire prevention personnel through the installation garrison mobile equipment department. Per reference (c), sufficient reserve vehicles shall be provided and maintained to replace out of service front line units. Reserve vehicles shall not be staffed except when used as replacements for front line apparatus or during major emergencies. Emergency vehicles are authorized to have appropriate emergency lights and warning devices, radios, and communications equipment installed. Emergency vehicles shall be maintained on a scheduled basis and repairs completed promptly to ensure they are reliable and ready for service.

12. <u>Information Technology Systems</u>. Information technology support is required for fire and emergency services departments to prepare and maintain incident reports, personnel records, training records, equipment inventories, physical fitness tests, and fire prevention inspection reports. HQMC (LFF) is developing the capability for an enterprise records management and reporting system for the Marine Corps structural and ARFF Fire and Emergency Services Departments. Until the enterprise solution is implemented, installation Fire and Emergency Services Departments shall ensure records management and reporting requirements are met using current capabilities, and are in compliance with references (i), (j) and (k).

13. <u>Technical Resources</u>. Fire and emergency services departments shall maintain a library of current directives, codes, publications, training materials, and orders necessary to manage the fire protection and emergency services program. Use of electronic libraries is encouraged.

14. <u>Mutual Aid Agreements</u>. Fire and emergency services departments are authorized and encouraged to enter into mutual aid agreements with local fire and emergency services jurisdictions where it is in the best interest of both parties. In the absence of formal mutual aid agreements, installation commanders may provide emergency assistance under their Immediate Response Authority per reference (l). Fire and emergency services departments are prohibited from increasing staffing or equipment solely to support mutual aid requirements. Any mutual aid service performed by Fire and Emergency Services Department personnel shall constitute service rendered in the line of duty. Mutual aid agreements shall be reviewed and updated at least every three years. Appendices B and C provide sample mutual aid agreements for both reimbursable and non-reimbursable support.

15. <u>Emergency Medical Services</u>. Fire and emergency services departments shall provide emergency medical service and emergency ambulance transport at Marine Corps installations upon written agreement with the Bureau of Medicine and Surgery (BUMED). Where BUMED personnel remain the primary EMS provider, Marine Corps fire and emergency services departments shall supplement and reinforce the EMS system. Fire and emergency services departments providing ambulance services are encouraged to provide Advanced Life Support capability.

16. <u>Hazardous Materials and Chemical, Biological, Radiological, Nuclear and High-Yield Explosive (CBRNE) Emergency Services</u>. Fire and emergency services departments shall provide hazardous materials and CBRNE emergency services in

accordance with Standard 471 of reference (a) and with reference (m). All Class A Marine Corps Fire & Emergency Services Departments shall provide Offensive Operation Hazardous Materials/CBRNE response capability in accordance with the Level of Service Objective - Operations, per reference (c), Table E3.T1.

17. <u>Specialized Rescue Services</u>. Fire and emergency services departments shall provide specialized rescue services (water rescue, dive rescue, vehicle rescue, confined space/trench rescue, high/low angle rescue) when hazards at the installation require these capabilities. Confined space rescue requirements shall be in accordance with reference (n).

18. <u>Fire and Emergency Services Department Awards</u>. Fire and emergency services departments are encouraged to reward outstanding personnel, departments, heroic actions and innovative programs. Fire and emergency services departments are encouraged to actively participate in the annual DoD Fire and Emergency Service Awards Program.

19. <u>Fire and Emergency Services Department Occupational Health And Safety Program</u>. The program shall be in accordance with Standard 1500 of reference (a) and per references (c) and (d), and shall include infectious disease control programs, medical surveillance, training, physical fitness/wellness and illness/injury prevention. Fire and emergency services departments shall monitor injury and illness trends, analyze data to focus loss prevention efforts and implement loss prevention initiatives. Per Standard 1500 of reference (a), each Fire and Emergency Services Department shall appoint a Safety Officer that meets the qualifications of Standard 1521 of reference (a). The role of Safety Officer may be filled by an existing position in the Fire and Emergency Services Department, such as the Training Officer, as an additional assigned duty.

20. <u>Fire and Emergency Services Department Program Assessments</u>. HQMC (LFF) shall provide Program Assessments on a three year cycle. This reporting requirement is exempt from reports control according to reference (i), Part IV, paragraph 7.k. The assessments provide a detailed analysis and evaluation of the fire and emergency services department programs, mission capability and status of each Fire and Emergency Services Department's self assessment efforts per reference (o). The assessment reports may be utilized to meet Inspector General of the Marine Corps Inspection and Assessment requirements. Installations shall prepare responses to each recommendation in the assessment report, indicating concurrence, non-concurrence or clarification. Responses shall include descriptions of when deficient conditions were, or will be, corrected. Installations shall submit responses to HQMC (LFF) within 60 days after receiving an assessment report.

Chapter 2

Fire and Emergency Services Department Training

1. <u>General</u>. The Fire and Emergency Services Department training program shall ensure that all personnel can operate in a safe and effective manner. Training programs shall be developed and implemented in accordance with references (a) and (g). Proficiency training shall be conducted on a recurring basis in order to maintain operational efficiency.

2. <u>Fire Fighting Training</u>. The International Fire Service Training Association (IFSTA) training manuals and DoD Fire and Emergency Services Certification System materials shall be used for basic fire fighter training. Local and regional fire schools shall also be used to supplement the fire fighter training and to provide advanced level training.

3. <u>Fire Prevention Training</u>. Codes 1 and 101 (Uniform Fire and Life Safety Codes) of reference (a) shall be used for basic fire prevention training. Additional training is recommended for public fire education, fire protection plan review, and fire protection system acceptance testing and maintenance.

4. <u>Administrative and Management Training</u>. Executive and personnel management training is required for Chief Officers. The National Fire Academy is one available source for this training. Incident Command System training is required for all Assistant Fire Chiefs of Operations, Deputy Fire Chiefs and Fire Chiefs in accordance reference (p) and paragraph 12 of this chapter. Fire Service college degrees or related college degrees are encouraged for Chief Officers.

5. <u>Professional Certification</u>. All department personnel shall participate in the DoD Fire and Emergency Services Certification Program per reference (g). Reciprocity for state and local training certifications is encouraged.

6. <u>Emergency Medical Training</u>. All emergency response personnel shall be trained and certified to the Department of Transportation First Responder level or to an equivalent level of emergency medical training. Full-time emergency response personnel (crew chiefs and fire fighters) shall be trained and certified to the Emergency Medical Technician level. Emergency Medical Technician certification is not required for emergency response personnel hired or promoted into a GS-0081 position prior to September 1986.

7. <u>Hazardous Materials Response Training</u>. All emergency response personnel shall be trained and certified to the Operations level in accordance with Standard 472 of reference (a) and with reference (q). All Class A Fire & Emergency Services Departments shall have an appropriate number of trained personnel at the Technician and Incident Commander levels to provide offensive (Level 3) response per Standard 471 of reference (a). Hazardous Materials Response Teams shall be equipped with Level A personal protective equipment.

8. <u>Chemical, Biological, Radiological, Nuclear, and High Level Explosives (CBRNE) Training</u>. All emergency response personnel shall receive CBRNE training, including but not be limited to: familiarization of CBRNE incidents and necessary measures to protect the responders while stabilizing an incident. All Class A Fire and Emergency Services Departments shall have sufficient personnel trained at the Technician and Incident Commander levels to provide offensive (Level 3) response per Standard 471 of reference (a).

9. <u>Specialized Rescue Training</u>. Fire & emergency services departments that provide specialized rescue capabilities (water rescue, dive rescue, heavy rescue, confined space/trench rescue, high/low angle rescue) shall ensure adequate personnel are properly trained for their rescue mission.

10. <u>Wildland Fire Training</u>. Fire and emergency services departments that provide wildland fire operations shall ensure sufficient emergency response personnel are trained for their expected level of involvement in the wildland fire mission. Wildland fire training shall support the installation Wildland Fire Management Plan. At a minimum, fire and emergency services wildland fire fighters shall be trained to Wildland Fire Fighter I per Standard 1051 of reference (a), National Wildfire Coordinating Group (NWCG) Fire Fighter II or equivalent level training.

11. <u>Driver/Operator Training</u>. All fire & emergency services driver/operators shall be trained and certified in the proper operation of the Fire and Emergency Services Department vehicles. Drivers/operators shall successfully complete an Emergency Vehicle Operators Course (EVOC) prior to operating the emergency vehicles.

12. <u>National Incident Management System (NIMS) Training</u>. To meet the DoD implementation of reference (p), all fire and emergency services personnel shall complete IS-700, NIMS: An Introduction; IS-800, National Response Plan; ICS-100, Introduction to Incident Command System; and ICS-200, Basic Incident Command System; or equivalent level training. Chief Officers shall also complete ICS-300, Intermediate Incident Command System and ICS-400, Advanced Incident Command System.

13. <u>Training Facilities</u>. Fire training facilities shall be provided to each installation fire & emergency services department to provide realistic proficiency training. Combining training facilities for adjoining DoD installations and use of regional training facilities should be considered as long as Marine Corps Fire & Emergency Services Department training needs are met. Facilities that support conduct of live fire training shall meet the requirements of Standard 1403 of reference (a).

14. <u>Administration</u>. The Fire Chief is responsible for the overall Fire and Emergency Services Department training program. The Fire Chief may appoint a senior officer as the Training Officer who is responsible for managing and conducting the training program. The Fire and Emergency Services Department Training Officer is recommended for appointment as the Fire and Emergency Services Department Safety Officer.

15. <u>Training Records</u>. The fire & emergency services department shall maintain individual training records for all training received by the fire & emergency services department personnel. All fire and emergency training records shall be maintained per reference (j) SSIC 11320.10, and in accordance with paragraph 12 of chapter 1.

Chapter 3

Fire and Emergency Services Department Operations

1. Structural Fire Response. Fire companies shall be dispatched on a first alarm assignment to meet the Minimum Level of Service Objectives - Operations, per reference (c), Table E3.T1. Class A fire and emergency services departments shall dispatch at least one ladder company on an initial full alarm assignment. Fire and Emergency Services Departments with water tower equipped engine companies shall establish flexible response procedures for utilizing the water tower equipped engines as either an engine or ladder company. Where ladder companies or water tower equipped engines companies are not available, an engine company may provide the ladder company requirement.

2. Aircraft Mishap Response. Fire and emergency services departments shall provide fire suppression, rescue, and medical assistance at aircraft mishaps in order to mitigate imminent danger to life and health threats. Upon arrival of the Air Station/Air Facility ARFF Section responders, the fire and emergency services department shall support the ARFF Section response and investigation efforts.

3. Hazardous Materials/CBRNE Response. Fire & emergency services department initial response to hazardous materials emergencies shall be in accordance with the Minimum Level of Service Objectives - Operations, per reference (c), Table E3.T1, and the Installation Oil and Hazardous Substance Spill Contingency Plan. All Fire and Emergency Services Departments shall be capable of hazard recognition, area isolation, personnel evacuation, substance identification, and initial incident command. Fire & emergency services departments with Hazardous Materials Incident Response Teams shall have the capability of Level A entry, in accordance with Standard 471 or reference (a), for rescue, material identification, control, and containment and mitigation purposes. Fire and Emergency Services Departments shall not be responsible for hazardous materials clean-up and disposal, but shall maintain procedures to alert the applicable local authorities of all suspect releases that may require clean-up and disposal.

4. Emergency Medical and Rescue Response. Fire and Emergency Services Department initial response to medical and rescue emergencies shall provide for prompt extrication and treatment of victims. Medical emergencies shall be handled in accordance with appropriate emergency medical protocols.

5. Wildland Fire Response. Fire and Emergency Services Department response to wildland fires shall be in accordance with the Installation Wild Fire Management Plan. The Fire and Emergency Services Department response shall be sufficient to ensure, to the greatest extent possible, that the wildland fire does not leave the installation property.

6. Disaster Response. Fire and Emergency Services Department response to natural or man-made disasters shall be in accordance with the Installation Disaster Response Plans. The response plans shall be coordinated with surrounding jurisdictions and shall be tested at least once a year.

7. Incident Command Systems. Incident command procedures shall be developed and utilized for all emergency incidents to provide for planned and systematic utilization of resources and shall be compliant with the National Incident Management System (NIMS), in accordance with reference (p).

8. <u>Emergency Communications</u>. Communications and dispatch systems are the important link in the emergency operation. Communication centers shall include two-way radio capability on multiple frequencies, direct communication lines with other emergency response organizations, central fire alarm receiver, voice recorder, public address, and paging capabilities and emergency backups.

9. <u>Standard Operating Procedures and Pre-Incident Plans</u>. Standard operating procedures shall be developed to improve operational performance by providing uniformity in practices, establishing responsibility, and enhancing accountability. Pre-incident plans shall be developed for all target hazards to ensure emergency response procedures are conducted as safely, effectively, and efficiently as possible.

10. <u>Personal Protective Equipment and Clothing</u>. All emergency response personnel shall be provided with appropriate protective equipment and clothing necessary to protect personnel from fire fighting, rescue, and hazardous materials exposure hazards. Personal protective equipment and clothing shall comply with appropriate standards of reference (a). All personnel involved in fire fighting and emergency operations shall utilize self-contained breathing apparatus and all components of their fire fighting or hazardous materials response protective ensemble.

11. <u>Fire and Emergency Services Department Uniforms</u>. Fire and Emergency Services Department personnel shall wear uniforms which provide a professional appearance and do not interfere with emergency operations. Personnel shall wear uniforms meeting the requirements of Standard 1975 of reference (a).

Chapter 4

Fire Prevention Program

1. <u>General</u>. Each installation shall establish and maintain an effective and planned fire prevention program. Fire prevention programs shall consist of continuing public fire education for all installation personnel, identification and elimination of fire hazards, enforcement of fire regulations, adequate fire protection for facilities and activities, promotion of fire prevention campaigns throughout the year, first aid fire fighting training, and fire investigations. The fire prevention program requires the strong support of the installation commander.

2. <u>Standards</u>. Fire prevention regulations shall comply with Codes 1 and 101 (Uniform Fire and Life Safety Codes) of reference (a), and with reference (b).

3. <u>Public Fire and Injury Prevention Education</u>. Public fire and injury prevention education programs shall be provided per reference (c) to inform and motivate DoD personnel and their families who reside or work on DoD installations or in Government-leased facilities of their individual responsibilities in fire prevention. Educational programs may be extended to surrounding jurisdictions with which there are mutual aid agreements. Educational programs shall focus on fire safe procedures, elimination of fire hazards, reporting of fires and other emergencies, first aid fire fighting and proper fire escape planning. Installations are authorized to expend funds for public fire education materials including nominal value giveaways.

4. <u>Fire Protection Plan Review</u>. Qualified fire prevention personnel shall review and approve all plans and specifications for construction, repair, and alterations to buildings and facilities.

5. <u>Fire Prevention Inspections</u>. Qualified fire prevention personnel will manage the inspection program and inspect all target hazards. Fire prevention personnel will report and ensure prompt correction of fire hazards as part of the installation hazard abatement plan. Inspection frequency shall be based on fire and life hazards, occupancy classification, fire loading, and importance of normal activity. All facilities shall be inspected at least semi-annually with more frequent inspections authorized for higher hazard facilities. Additional inspections are authorized to ensure prompt correction of all life safety related deficiencies and all facility deficiencies in ordinary, special, or extra hazard occupancies as defined in references (a) and (b).

6. <u>Permits</u>. High fire hazard activities shall be regulated through a permit system. All precautions specified by the fire permit shall be employed to minimize the risk of high fire hazard activities.

7. <u>Public Assembly Facilities</u>. Public assembly facility managers shall be trained in proper fire prevention responsibilities due to the high life loss potential at these facilities. Managers shall notify the Fire and Emergency Services Department when planning large social events involving extensive decorations, large crowds, or unusual arrangements.

8. <u>Key Access Boxes</u>. Where access to facilities is restricted because of secured openings or where immediate access is necessary for life saving purposes, key access boxes with access keys are authorized. Per reference (a), Key Access Boxes shall be approved by the Authority Having Jurisdiction

(AHJ) and shall be consistent throughout the installation. The Installation Fire Chief serves as the AHJ for approving key access boxes used on his/her installation(s).

9. Family Housing. A fire prevention orientation program shall be provided for all new housing occupants. Housing units shall be inspected when directed by the installation commander.

10. Contractor Operations. Fire prevention personnel shall attend pre-construction meetings to coordinate fire prevention requirements with installation contractors. All construction projects, repair, and maintenance work and service contract work shall be monitored by fire prevention personnel. Unsafe conditions shall be reported promptly to the contracting officer for corrective action.

11. Fire Warden Program. Each installation Fire and Emergency Services Department shall designate a Fire Warden to help execute the fire prevention program. The Fire Warden may appoint additional Fire Wardens for designated buildings and facilities. Fire Wardens are responsible for the day to day fire prevention regulations within their designated building and facilities. The Fire Warden shall inform the Fire Chief in writing of all Fire Warden assignments. All Fire Wardens shall receive fire prevention training from the fire prevention staff.

Chapter 5

Fire Protection Engineering

1. <u>Standards</u>. Fire protection engineering criteria shall conform to references (a) and (b). The Factory Mutual Loss Prevention Data Sheets, International Building Code, and fire protection criteria from DoD and HQMC also provide specific fire protection guidance.

2. <u>Surveys</u>. Qualified Fire Protection Engineers (as defined in reference (b)) shall survey installations on a five year cycle. Surveys should be conducted in-house by qualified personnel, or be contracted locally. If necessary, installations may submit a funding request for surveys via a prioritized centrally managed program (P1) funding submission. Naval Facilities Engineering Command Fire Protection Engineers are the recommended source for conducting surveys. Fire protection surveys provide a highly technical review of the life safety features, fire protection systems, and physical features of facilities at the installation. Fire Protection Engineering Survey Reports shall receive prompt attention and deficiencies should be corrected as soon as possible. Survey reports and activity corrective action plans shall be submitted to CMC (LFF) within 60 days after receiving the survey to facilitate HQMC project validation and funding. This reporting requirement is exempt from reports control according to reference (i), part IV, paragraph 7.k.

3. <u>Fire Protection Projects</u>. Fire protection facility projects shall be submitted to HQMC in accordance with reference (r) in order to correct deficiencies which exceed local approval authority. Projects that are driven entirely by fire protection requirements; that use new fire protection technologies; or that involve unique and complex fire protection designs shall be reviewed by CMC (LFF-1). The installation Fire & Emergency Services Department, in conjunction with the Public Works Department, shall prepare appropriate project documentation for all fire protection facility projects.

4. <u>Fire Protection Systems Maintenance</u>. Maintenance of fire protection systems shall comply with reference (s).

5. <u>Residential Sprinklers</u>. Automatic residential sprinklers are required for all new multi-family housing occupancies as defined by reference (b). This includes bachelor enlisted quarters (BEQs), bachelor officer quarters (BOQs), and dormitories and lodges as per reference (t). Sprinklers are also required for all whole house renovations of existing multi-family housing projects.

6. <u>Barracks Sprinklers</u>. In accordance with reference (r), in the case that a barracks is taken off line for a major repair, the installation of a fire sprinkler system is mandatory as part of the repair for those barracks regardless of the ratio of repair costs to replacement costs of the facility. If there is any reason the installation of a fire sprinkler system should not occur during a major repair then the installation must submit a request for waiver or exemption to CMC (LFF) for consideration and final determination.

Chapter 6

Aircraft Rescue and Fire Fighting

1. <u>Standards</u>. ARFF requirements shall conform to reference (u), which defines the ARFF missions at specified airfields. The staffing and equipping of the ARFF Section shall be in accordance with reference (u).

2. <u>Vehicles</u>. Primary ARFF fire fighting vehicles and capabilities are defined in reference (u). In addition to the primary fire fighting vehicles, ARFF Sections require support vehicles for rescue, re-supply, and incident command.

3. <u>Uniforms</u>. All ARFF personnel shall wear a fire resistant uniform underneath their Proximity Fire Fighting Gear. Due to availability and costs, aviation flight suits are an acceptable uniform for ARFF personnel.

4. <u>Inspections</u>. ARFF Sections shall be inspected in accordance with the local Commanding General's Inspection Program to ensure mission readiness. Other inspections include the Inspector General of the Marine Corps and Naval Safety Center surveys.

5. <u>Training</u>. References (u) and (v) establish training requirements for ARFF personnel (Military Occupational Specialty (MOS) 7002/7051). ARFF Marines shall maintain a continuous training cycle to keep up with the latest technology and required certifications for their assigned position.

6. <u>Self Assessment</u>. Air Station/Air Facility ARFF Sections shall establish goals and procedures for completing self assessments using procedures outlined in reference (o).

Chapter 7

Reporting and Investigations

1. Fire and Emergency Incident Reporting. Fire and Emergency Services Incident Response Reports will be prepared and submitted in accordance with reference (c). Reports will be prepared using the National Fire Incident Reporting System (NFIRS) software and submitted to the U.S. Fire Administration within 60 days of the incident. Report Control Symbol DD-11320-01 External RCS DD-AT&L(AR)1765 is assigned to this reporting requirement.

2. Large Loss Initial Incident Reports. An initial report shall be made within 24 hours for all fires or related emergencies that cause damage of $100,000 or more, are of unusual origin, or result in loss of life or serious injury to personnel. The report message shall be transmitted by the installation to CMC (LFF) via the normal chain of command. A template Large Loss Initial Incident Report is included at Appendix D. Report Control Symbol DD-11320-01 External RCS DD-AT&L(AR)1765 is assigned to this reporting requirement.

3. Fire Investigations. All fires shall be investigated by the fire and emergency services department to determine probable origin and cause and to reveal lessons learned to support local fire prevention and protection improvements. Fires which may involve criminal activity shall be reported promptly to the Naval Criminal Investigative Service. Fires involving loss of life, multiple serious injuries, property damage estimates exceeding $100,000, failure of fire protection systems, fire bombings, fire sabotage of critical operations, or incidents where an independent investigation is in the best interest of the Marine Corps, shall be reported to CMC (LFF) via the normal chain of command within 24 hours of the incident.

Appendix A

Definitions

Aerial Ladder - A fire fighting emergency response vehicle equipped with a mechanically operated ladder and turntable, a compliment of portable ground ladders and various rescue, ventilation, salvage, and overhaul tools.

Aircraft Rescue and Fire Fighting Branch - The primary Marine Corps organization responsible for providing fire suppression and rescue to aircraft incidents.

Apparatus - Specially designed emergency response vehicles which provide equipment and materials necessary for fire fighting and emergency services. Apparatus includes pumpers, aerial ladders, and rescue vehicles.

Automatic Sprinkler System - A fire extinguishing system with pipes and automatically activating heads which distribute water or water based extinguishing agents over a fire area.

Cross Staffing - Utilizing the personnel from one staffed company to staff multiple companies.

Disaster Response - That portion of the emergency services program which deals with control and mitigation of unforeseen incidents which exceeds the normal capabilities of the affected installation or jurisdiction.

Driver/Operator - Fire and Emergency Services Department personnel trained and certified in the proper checkout, maintenance, and operation of Fire and Emergency Services Department apparatus.

Emergency Medical Protocols - The procedures and regulations governing the emergency medical treatment of specific injuries and illnesses.

Emergency Medical Services - The portion of the emergency services program which provides rapid and quality care to people who are suffering from sudden injury or illness.

Emergency Medical Technician - The second level of Fire and Emergency Services Department emergency medical service certification. The Emergency Medical Technician is trained in pre-hospital life support and patient transportation.

Emergency Services Program - A comprehensive approach to control and mitigate damages from natural or man-made incidents.

Emergency Response Personnel - Fire and Emergency Services Department personnel trained and responsible for performing hazardous fire fighting and emergency service missions.

Emergency Vehicle Operators Course (EVOC) - A training course designed to provide the skills and knowledge necessary to properly and safely operate Fire and Emergency Services Department apparatus and emergency response vehicles.

Engine Company - A compliment of emergency response personnel staffing a Fire and Emergency Services Department pumper. The engine company's primary role during fire incidents is establishing a water supply and delivering water through hose lines to control the fires.

First-Aid Fire Fighting - Initial fire suppression activities conducted by non-Fire and Emergency Services Department personnel generally utilizing portable fire extinguishers.

Fire and Emergency Services Incident Reports - Data complied on each incident to determine trends, evaluate effectiveness of the fire protection and emergency services programs, and indicate areas needing improvement.

Fire Brigade - An organization consisting of installation personnel trained to provide fire fighting and fire prevention activities within the installation.

Fire and Emergency Services Department - The primary Marine Corps organization responsible for providing fire protection and emergency services to the installation and surrounding jurisdictions.

Fire and Emergency Services Communications - The ability to effectively receive calls for assistance from telephone, radio, or fire alarm receiving equipment, process the calls, dispatch the appropriate emergency response vehicles, provide relevant information, and request additional assistance.

Fire and Emergency Services Safety Officer - The fire and emergency services person assigned by the Fire Chief to manage the fire & emergency services department safety and health program. The Safety Officer shall have direct access to the Fire Chief and shall have the authority to cause immediate correction of situations that create an imminent hazard to personnel.

Fire and Emergency Services Training Officer - The fire & emergency services person assigned by the Fire Chief to manage the training program. In larger fire and emergency services departments, the Assistant Fire Chief of Training is assigned as the Training Officer.

Fire Extinguishing System - A fire protection system which automatically controls and suppresses fires including automatic sprinkler systems, dry chemical systems, and foam systems.

Fire Flow - The amount of water necessary to confine and extinguish fires in facilities which represents large fire loss potential.

Fire Investigation - An examination of the fire scene to determine the cause and origin of the fire, any special circumstance surrounding the fire, and to develop lesson learned. A fire investigation may also serve as the basis for a criminal investigation if the fire is determined to be of incendiary or suspicious origin.

Fire Loading - The amount of combustibles within a space or building.

Fire Permit - An official document issued by the fire & emergency services department which allows for the use, handling, storage, occupancy, or control of specific hazardous operations or conditions.

Fire Prevention - The portion of the fire protection program which seeks to prevent the outbreak of fire through education, inspection, enforcement, and investigation.

Fire Prevention Orientation Program - A public fire education program for all new installation housing occupants which addresses fire escape planning, fire and emergency reporting, home fire hazards, smoke detectors, and other fire protection features.

<u>Fire Prevention Personnel</u> - Fire and emergency services department personnel trained and responsible for administering the fire prevention program.

<u>Fire Protection Engineering</u> - The portion of the fire protection program which deals with the study, design, and installation of fire protection and life safety systems.

<u>Fire Protection Facility Projects</u> - A single planned undertaking of construction, alteration, repair or maintenance necessary to improve the fire protection or life safety characteristics of a building, structure, or other real property.

<u>Fire Protection Plan Review</u> - A fire prevention strategy involving the review of building design plans and specifications to ensure fire protection and life safety requirements are satisfied.

<u>Fire Protection Program</u> - A comprehensive approach to control and mitigate damages from hostile fires including ignition prevention, slowing fire growth and spread, detection and alarm, suppression, confinement, and evacuation of occupants.

<u>Fire Protection Specialists</u> - Fire and Emergency Services Department personnel trained and responsible for one specific portion of the fire protection and emergency services program such as the public fire education program.

<u>Fire Protection Systems</u> - Equipment installed in buildings and other structures designed to detect fires, provide alarm indication of fires, or extinguish fires.

<u>Fire Protection System Acceptance Testing</u> - A fire prevention strategy involving the testing of newly installed or renovated fire protection systems to ensure the systems are operating properly.

<u>Fire Suppression</u> - The portion of the fire protection program which deals with the control and extinguishment of fires through automatic or manual means.

<u>Fire Warden</u> - Designated individuals within each installation department who are responsible for executing and implementing the fire prevention program within their department, building, facility, or unit.

<u>Flexible Response</u> - A Fire and Emergency Services Department response methodology utilizing water tower equipment pumpers as either an engine company or a truck company.

<u>Halon</u> - A fire extinguishing agent which utilizes fluorine, chlorine, bromine or iodine based hydrocarbons to interfere with the combustion process. Halon has been identified as an ozone depleting substance.

<u>Hazardous Materials Emergency Response</u> - The portion of the emergency service program which deals with the control and mitigation of spills and releases involving hazardous materials or substances.

<u>Hazardous Materials Incident Response Team</u> - Teams which are organized, trained, and equipped to respond to Level 3 hazardous materials incidents and to utilize Level A Personnel Protective Equipment per Standard 471 of reference (a).

Hose Stream Demand - The amount of water necessary in conjunction with automatic sprinklers to effect final extinguishment of fires and provide exposure protection.

Incident - An occurrence or event, either man-made or natural, which requires action by emergency services personnel to prevent or minimize loss of life, damage to property, or destruction of natural resources.

Incident Command System - The combination of facilities, equipment, personnel, procedures and communications operating within a common organizational structure with responsibility for the management of assigned resources to effectively accomplish stated objectives pertaining to an incident.

Infectious Disease Control - A comprehensive approach to manage the risks associated with infectious and communicable diseases which are designed to prevent infection from occurring in both patients and emergency care providers.

Installation Disaster Response Plan - The installation's comprehensive plan to mitigate the damage from a disaster and to sustain emergency services during the disaster.

Installation Fire Management Plan - The installation's comprehensive plan to protect the base, mission, personnel, natural resources, and wildlife from fires with emphasis on the wildland fire threats.

Installation Hazard Abatement Plan - An installation's systematic program to correct or reduce hazardous conditions in accordance with reference (w).

Installation Oil and Hazardous Substance Spill Contingency Plans - The installation's comprehensive response plans to oil and hazardous substances spills as required by reference (x).

Interservice Support - Support provided by one DoD activity to a DoD activity of another Military Service, Defense Agency, Unified Combatant Command, Army Reserves, Navy Reserves, Air Force Reserves, Marine Corps Reserves, Air National Guard, or Field Activity.

Interservice Support Agreement - An agreement to provide recurring support to another DoD or non-DoD Federal activity. Support agreements are recorded on a DD Form 1144, or a similar format (e.g., computer generated DD Form 1144). They define the support to be provided by one supplier to one or more receivers, specify the basis for calculating reimbursement charges (if any) for each service, establish the billing and reimbursement process, and specify other terms and conditions of the agreement.

Ladder Company - A compliment of emergency response personnel staffing a fire & emergency services department aerial ladder. The ladder company's roles during fire incidents include, but are not limited to: elevated access and rescue, elevated master streams, search and rescue, ventilation, utility control, salvage and overhaul.

Multi-family Housing - A residential building with more than two living units under one roof.

Mutual Aid Agreement - A formal agreement between surrounding jurisdictions and the installation to provide supplemental Fire and Emergency Services Department assistance when requested by either the jurisdiction or the installation. See Appendices B and C for examples of mutual aid agreements.

Occupancy Classification - The grouping of buildings or portion of buildings based on their use or intended use.

Ozone Depleting Substances - Substances which can destroy the stratospheric ozone layer and thus increase the amount of ultraviolet light reaching the earth's surface. The use of Ozone Depleting Substances is strictly regulated by DoD and the Environmental Protection Agency.

Position Staffing Factor - The factor utilized to determine emergency response staffing requirements. The factor is based on a 24-hour Fire and Emergency Services Department shift, a 72-hour work week, and includes an adjustment for non-available time (annual leave, sick leave, other leave).

Pre-incident Plans - Fire & emergency services department plans for fighting a fire in a target hazard.

Public Fire Education - A fire prevention strategy which seeks to improve human fire safety behavior through the teaching and disseminating of fire protection information.

Pumper - A fire fighting emergency response vehicle capable of carrying hose, transporting water, and pumping water.

Rescue Apparatus - An emergency response vehicle capable of transporting specialized rescue equipment.

Residential Sprinkler System - An automatic sprinkler system designed for homes and living quarters which will provide early warning and suppression of residential fires.

Response Time - The time required by the fire and emergency services department to respond to an incident starting with the receipt of the emergency alarm and ending when the emergency vehicles arrive at the incident location.

Risk Analysis - A study of the elements which pose a hazardous situation to assess the probability and severity of an incident prior to devising a means of controlling the hazardous situation.

Self-Contained Breathing Apparatus (SCBA) - A self-contained breathing air system designed to allow emergency services personnel to enter hazardous or oxygen deficient atmospheres.

Specialized Rescue Response - The portion of the emergency services program which removes victims from hazardous or life threatening conditions to areas of safety or treatment.

Standard Operating Procedures - The procedures and regulations governing emergency operations to provide uniformity in practices, establish responsibility and enhance accountability.

Target Hazards - Buildings, structures or other facilities which pose high fire risks due to their size, value, strategic importance, life threat or fire hazards.

Wildland Fire Apparatus - An emergency response vehicle capable of transporting water, pumping water, and carrying equipment used for wildland or brush fires.

<u>Water Tower</u> - A Fire and Emergency Services Department pumper equipped with a hydraulically operated, telescopic boom. The boom is equipped with a waterway and an extension ladder for emergency escape purposes.

Appendix B

Mutual Aid Agreement (Reimbursable)

THIS AGREEMENT, made and entered into this____day of _____, 20__ by and between the (Municipality/State Agency/Federal Agency) and the Department of the Navy, through (Marine Corps Installation), pursuant to 42 U.S.C. 1856a, shall serve as the agreement between the parties for mutual aid fire protection and emergency services.

WITNESETH:

All prior agreements between the parties hereto are hereby superseded and canceled.

WHEREAS, the (Marine Corps Installation) is located within the corporate limits of the (Municipality/State), and

Or

WHEREAS, the lands or districts of the parties hereto are adjacent or contiguous so that mutual assistance in an emergency situation is deemed feasible and desirable; and

WHEREAS, both parties maintain equipment and personnel for the suppression of fires, rescue, emergency medical services and response to hazardous materials incidents within their respective jurisdictions; and

WHEREAS, the parties desire to augment the fire protection and associated emergency services available in their respective jurisdictions; and

WHEREAS, this mutual aid agreement is in the best interests of all parties;

THEREFORE THE PARTIES AGREE:

I. PROVISIONS OF RESPONSE

1. Marine Corps Installation

a. (Marine Corps Installation) agrees to provide fire equipment response to alarms of fire or other emergencies to the (Municipality/State Agency/Federal Agency) where the (Municipal/State Agency/Federal Agency) Fire and Emergency Services Department requests such assistance. This response will be commensurate with the scope of the emergency involved and to the extent that limitations of forces available at the time of the occurrence will permit.

b. In the event (Marine Corps Installation) Emergency Communications Center receives an alarm of fire or other emergency call involving non-Marine Corps property, the alarm will be immediately relayed to the (Municipal/State Agency/Federal Agency) Emergency Communications Center.

2. (Municipality/State Agency/Federal Agency)

a. The (Municipality/State Agency/Federal Agency) agrees to provide fire equipment response to alarms of fire or other emergencies to the (Marine Corps Installation) or to other military or defense establishments protected by the (Marine Corps Installation) Fire and Emergency Services Department, where the (Marine Corps Installation) Fire and Emergency Services Department requests such assistance. This response will be commensurate with the scope of the emergency involved and to the extent that limitations of forces available at the time of the occurrence will permit.

b. In the event the (Municipal/State Agency/Federal Agency) Emergency Communications Center receives an alarm of fire or other emergency call involving government property in the (Marine Corps Installation) area, the alarm will be immediately relayed to the (Marine Corps Installation) Emergency Communications Center.

3. Whenever the senior officer of the (Municipal/State Agency/Federal Agency) or the (Marine Corps Installation) Fire and Emergency Services Department determines it would be advisable to request emergency assistance, the senior officer on duty at the Fire and Emergency Services Department receiving the request shall take the following action:

a. Immediately determine if the requested apparatus and personnel are available to respond to the request, and

b. In accordance with the terms of this agreement, forthwith dispatch such apparatus and personnel as in the judgment of the senior officer receiving the call should be sent, with instructions as to their mission.

4. The Fire Chiefs of the respective Fire and Emergency Services Departments will formulate detailed response plans, to include automatic dispatching of mutual aid resources on first alarms, where appropriate.

5. The rendering of assistance under the terms of this agreement shall not be mandatory; however, the party receiving the request for assistance shall immediately inform the requesting party if assistance cannot be rendered.

6. The senior officer of the Fire and Emergency Services Department requesting assistance shall assume full command of the incident. However, under procedures agreed to by the senior officers of the Fire and Emergency Services Departments involved, a senior officer of the department furnishing the assistance may assume full command of the incident.

7. All officers and personnel of the Fire and Emergency Services Departments to this agreement are invited and encouraged, on a reciprocal basis, to frequently visit each other's activities for guided familiarization tours consistent with local security requirements and, as feasible, to jointly conduct pre-incident planning inspections, drills and training.

II. PROVISIONS OF CLAIMS AND REIMBURSEMENT

1. The parties hereto waive all claims against every other party for compensation resulting from any loss, damage, personal injury, or death occurring in consequence of the performance of this agreement.

2. The parties agree that the (Municipal/State Agency) Fire Service may file a claim with the Administrator of the United States Fire Administration for the costs incurred in fighting a fire on property that is under the jurisdiction of the United States, pursuant to 15 U.S.C. 2210.

3. Reimbursements between the (Marine Corps Installation) and the (Federal Agency) Fire and Emergency Services Departments shall comply with the Economy Act provisions, 31 U.S.C. 1535.

4. The parties agree that the initial response of like-kind resources (similar resources provided by both parties) shall not be reimbursed for responses of 24-hours or less in duration. For responses exceeding 24 hours duration, reimbursement for the assisting party's mutual aid resources shall cover the entire time of commitment, starting with the initial dispatch and ending when the personnel and apparatus return at their home location. Reimbursement of unlike kind resources (resources provided by only one party) shall be reimbursed for the entire time of the commitment, including the initial response.

5. The parties shall develop reimbursement cost procedures that detail the reimbursable and non-reimbursable costs and services, the reimbursement rates, cost sharing provisions and billing procedures. The reimbursement cost procedures shall be included as an addendum to this Agreement.

6. Disputes - Unresolvable differences concerning this mutual aid agreement shall be elevated for resolution through each party's chain of command to the signatories as the final arbiters.

III. TERMS OF AGREEMENT

This agreement shall become effective on the date of the last signature to the agreement and will remain in effect for three years from that date. Notification of the intention of either party to terminate the Agreement prior to that date will be in the form of a written submission to the other party at least 180 days in advance of the proposed date of termination.

IN WITNESS WHEREOF, the parties hereto have executed this agreement at (City, State) on the day and year first above written.

_____   _____
(Name)   (Name, Rank)
(Title)   Commanding Officer
(Federal/Municipality/State Agency)   (Marine Corps Installation)

Date: _____   Date: _____

_____   _____
(Name)   (Name)
Fire Chief   Fire Chief
(Federal/Municipality/State Agency)   (Marine Corps Installation)

Date: _____   Date: _____

Appendix C

Mutual Aid Agreement (Non-Reimbursable)

THIS AGREEMENT, made and entered into this_____day of _____, 20__ by and between the (Municipality/State Agency/Federal Agency)) and the Department of the Navy, through (Marine Corps Installation), pursuant to 42 U.S.C. 1856a, shall serve as the agreement between the parties for mutual aid fire protection and emergency services.

WITNESETH:

All prior agreements between the parties hereto are hereby superseded and canceled.

WHEREAS, the (Marine Corps Installation) is located within the corporate limits of the (Municipality/State), and

Or

WHEREAS, the lands or districts of the parties hereto are adjacent or contiguous so that mutual assistance in an emergency situation is deemed feasible; and

WHEREAS, both parties maintain equipment and personnel for the suppression of fires, rescue, emergency medical services and response to hazardous materials incidents within their respective jurisdictions; and

WHEREAS, the parties desire to augment the fire protection and associated services available in their respective jurisdictions; and

WHEREAS, this mutual aid agreement is in the best interests of all parties;

THEREFORE THE PARTIES AGREE:

I. PROVISIONS OF RESPONSE

1. Marine Corps Installation

a. (Marine Corps Installation) agrees to provide fire equipment response to alarms of fire or other emergencies to the (Municipality/State Agency/ Federal Agency) where the (Municipal/State Agency/Federal Agency) Fire and Emergency Services Department requests such assistance, at no cost when such assistance is requested by the (Municipality/State Agency/Federal Agency) Fire and Emergency Services Department. This response will be commensurate with the scope of the emergency involved and to the extent that limitations of forces available at the time of the occurrence will permit.

b. In the event (Marine Corps Installation) Emergency Communications Center receives an alarm of fire or other emergency call involving non-Marine Corps property, the alarm will be immediately relayed to the (Municipality/State Agency/Federal Agency) Emergency Communications Center.

2. (Municipality/State Agency/Federal Agency)

a. The (Municipality/State Agency/Federal Agency) agrees to provide fire equipment response to alarms of fire or other emergencies to the (Marine Corps Installation) or to other military or defense establishments, protected by the (Marine Corps Installation) Fire and Emergency Services Department, at no cost when such assistance is requested by the (Marine Corps Installation) Fire and Emergency Services Department. This response will be commensurate with the scope of the emergency involved and to the extent that limitations of forces available at the time of the occurrence will permit.

b. In the event the (Municipality/State Agency/Federal Agency) Emergency Communications Center receives an alarm of fire or other emergency call involving government property in the (Marine Corps Installation) area, the alarm will be immediately relayed to the (Marine Corps Installation) Emergency Communications Center.

3. Whenever the senior officer of the (Municipality/State Agency/Federal Agency) or the (Marine Corps Installation) Fire and Emergency Services Department determines it would be advisable to request emergency assistance, the senior officer on duty at the Fire and Emergency Services Department receiving the request shall take the following action:

a. Immediately determine if the requested apparatus and personnel are available to respond to the request, and

b. In accordance with the terms of this agreement, forthwith dispatch such apparatus and personnel as in the judgment of the senior officer receiving the call should be sent, with instructions as to their mission.

4. The Fire Chiefs of the respective Fire and Emergency Services Departments will formulate detailed response plans, to include automatic dispatching of mutual aid resources on first alarms, where appropriate.

5. The rendering of assistance under the terms of this agreement shall not be mandatory; however, the party receiving the request for assistance shall immediately inform the requesting service if assistance cannot be rendered.

6. The parties hereto waive all claims against every other party for compensation for any loss, damage, personal injury, or death occurring in consequence of the performance of this agreement.

7. It is agreed that the (Municipality/State Agency/Federal Agency) may file a claim with the Administrator of the United States Fire Administration for the costs incurred in fighting a fire on property which is under the jurisdiction of the United States, pursuant to 15 U.S.C. 2210.

8. The senior officer of the Fire and Emergency Services Department of the requesting service shall assume full command of the incident. However, under procedures agreed to by the senior officers of the Fire and Emergency Services Departments involved, a senior officer of the department furnishing the assistance may assume full command of the incident.

9. All officers and personnel of the Fire and Emergency Services Departments of the parties to this agreement are invited and encouraged, on a reciprocal basis, to frequently visit each other's activities for guided familiarization tours consistent with local security requirements and, as feasible, to jointly conduct pre-incident planning inspections, drills and training.

10. Disputes - Unresolvable differences concerning this mutual aid agreement shall be elevated for resolution through each party's chain of command to the signatories as the final arbiters.

II. TERMS OF AGREEMENT

This agreement shall become effective on the date of the last signature to the agreement and will remain in effect for three years from that date. Notification of the intention of either party to terminate the Agreement prior to that date will be in the form of a written submission to the other party at least 180 days in advance of the proposed date of termination.

IN WITNESS WHEREOF, the parties hereto have executed this agreement at (City, State) on the day and year first above written.

_____	_____
(Name)	(Name, Rank)
(Title)	Commanding Officer
(Federal/Municipality/State Agency)	(Marine Corps Installation)
Date: _____	Date: _____
_____	_____
(Name)	(Name)
Fire Chief	Fire Chief
(Federal/Municipality/State Agency)	(Marine Corps Installation)
Date: _____	Date: _____

Appendix D

Large Loss Initial Incident Report Sample Message

Use this format to report (within 24-hours) all fires or related emergencies that cause damage of $100,000 or more, are of unusual origin, or result in loss of life or serious injury to personnel. Where the requested information is not applicable or not relevant to the analysis of the fire, insert "not applicable."

(Precedence - Priority)

FROM   REPORTING INSTALLATION

TO   CMC WASHINGTON DC//LFF-1/APX-34 (IF APPLICABLE)//

INFO   CHAIN OF COMMAND

UNCLAS //N05102//FOUO (Normally unclassified unless classified information must be included.)

MSGID/GENADMIN/MSG ORIG/SER NO./MONTH//

SUBJ/LARGE LOSS INITIAL INCIDENT REPORT (REPORT CONTROL SYMBOL DD-11320-04)

AMPN/REF A/MCO P11000.11 MARINE CORPS FIRE PROTECTION AND EMERGENCY SERVICES PROGRAM//

NARR/FOR OFFICIAL USE ONLY. THIS IS A GENERAL USE SAFETY REPORT TO BE USED FOR SAFETY PURPOSES//

POC/NAME/RANK/PRIMARY PHONE/-/LOCATION/EMAIL//

RMKS/1. PER REF A, THE FOLLOWING INFORMATION IS SUBMITTED:

ALPHA:

    1. UIC OF REPORTING ACTIVITY:
    2. LOCAL DATE AND TIME OF FIRE OCCURRED:
    3. LOCATE DATE AND TIME FIRE UNDER CONTROL:
    4. GEOGRAPHICAL LOCATION: (Include city and state and whether on or off Marine Corps property. If on Marine Corps property, give name and UIC of installation where fire occurred.)

BRAVO: FIRE RELATED INJURIES:

    1. NAME/AGE/SEX: (If more than one person is injured, information in this section must be specific as to which individual is being described. Repeat items 1 through 3 for each individual.)
    2. RANK AND DESIGNATOR, OR RATE AND NEC, OR JOB TITLE, SERIES AND GRADE
    3. FATALITY OR EXTENT OR INJURY/ILLNESS: (Specify fatality, percentage of body burned, degree of burns, fractures, smoke inhalation, etc.)

CHARLIE: MATERIAL PROPERTY DAMAGE

    1. TYPE OF PROPERTY: (Structural, agricultural, automobile, ship, aircraft, etc.)
    2. ESTIMATED COST TO REPAIR OR REPLACE DOD PROPERTY:
    3. ESTIMATED COST TO REPAIR OR REPLACE NON-DOD PROPERTY:

4. FIRE EQUIPMENT DAMAGED: (fire apparatus, support equipment, etc.)

DELTA: NARRATIVE: State as much amplifying information as available. Include chain of events leading up to, through, and subsequent to the fire.